W9-BMV-510

PRESIDENTS
★ FACTS & FUN ★
ACTIVITY BOOK

LEN EPSTEIN

DOVER PUBLICATIONS, INC.
MINEOLA, NEW YORK

GREEN EDITION ®

At Dover Publications we're committed to producing books in an earth-friendly manner and to helping our customers make greener choices.

Manufacturing books in the United States ensures compliance with strict environmental laws and eliminates the need for international freight shipping, a major contributor to global air pollution. And printing on recycled paper helps minimize our consumption of trees, water and fossil fuels.

The text of this book was printed on paper made with 50% post-consumer waste and the cover was printed on paper made with 10% post-consumer waste. At Dover, we use Environmental Paper Network's Paper Calculator to measure the benefits of these choices, including: the number of trees saved, gallons of water conserved, as well as air emissions and solid waste eliminated.

Courier Corporation, the manufacturer of this book, owns the Green Edition Trademark.

Please visit the product page for *Presidents Facts and Fun Activity Book* at www.doverpublications.com to see a detailed account of the environmental savings we've achieved over the life of this book.

Note

Learn fascinating facts about the American presidents, and have fun as well! You'll find mazes, matching, spot the differences, and many other fun activities. [Note: A few of the presidents appear out of order because their activities need to fit on two facing pages.] When you're finished, you can enjoy coloring in the pages, too. You can use the list of the presidents and their terms in office on the inside back cover of the book for some of the activities.

Copyright

Copyright © 2012 by Dover Publications, Inc.
All rights reserved.

Bibliographical Note

Presidents Facts and Fun Activity Book is a new work, first published by Dover Publications in 2012.

International Standard Book Number

ISBN-13: 978-0-486-48277-4
ISBN-10: 0-486-48277-4

Manufactured in the United States by Courier Corporation
48277401
www.doverpublications.com

Help George find his teeth.

George Washington, the first American president, has lost his teeth! To find them, he has to travel through towns and farmlands. He'll see everything from Betsy Ross to an alien. Can you help him? When he does find them, tell him not to forget to brush!

Where's the new White House?

John Adams, the second president, was the first to live in the White House as we know it today. When he moved in with his wife, Abigail, it wasn't finished yet and was called the "Presidential Palace." Can you help Adams find his way to the White House?

What's the difference?

Thomas Jefferson, the third president, wrote the Declaration of Independence in June 1776. He rented the second floor of a house on Market Street owned by Jacob Graff. The house still stands today. Find and circle 10 things in the bottom picture that are different from the top one.

3

Find the brains!

James Madison, the fourth president, is known as the "Father of the Constitution," although he said that it took several brains to put the document together! Find and circle 10 brains that are hidden in the picture.

Find what's missing.

James Monroe was the fifth American president. He is best known for his "Monroe Doctrine," a policy of the United States stating that we would stay out of European quarrels as long as they didn't interfere in North or South America. Find and circle 10 things in the bottom picture that are different from the top one.

John Quincy Adams's maze.

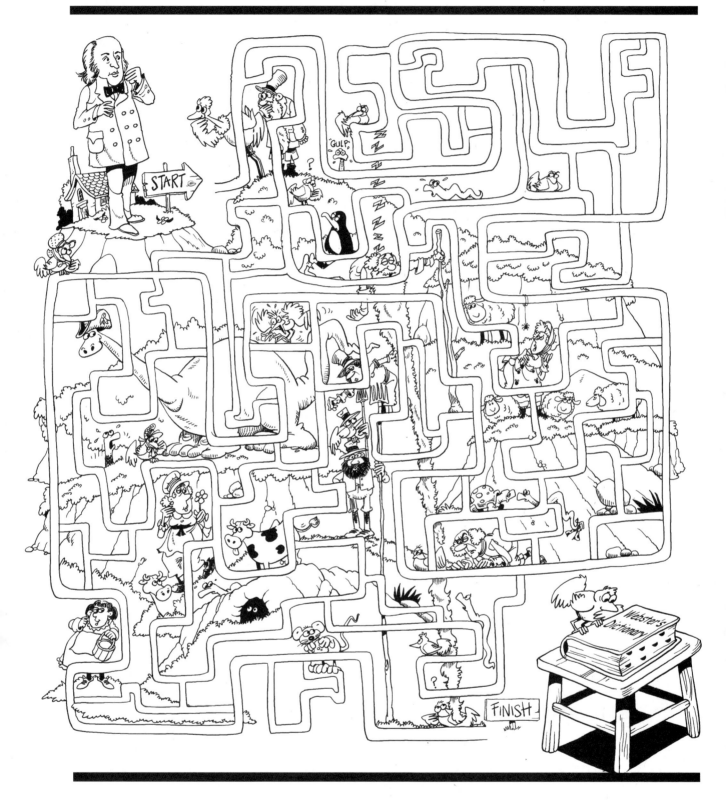

John Quincy Adams, the sixth president, was the first president whose father was also president. During his term of office, *Webster's Dictionary* was published. Can you help President Adams get to his new dictionary?

What's missing?

Andrew Jackson, the seventh president, was born in a log cabin. He fought in several battles and earned the nickname "Old Hickory" for being brave and tough. Find and circle 10 things in the picture on the right that are different from the picture on the left.

Find the bag of gold!

Martin Van Buren, the eighth president, was known as a great politician. He worked hard to make the country prosperous. In this picture, Van Buren is looking for the bag of gold that he lost. Find and circle it.

Find the whale oil lamp.

William Henry Harrison, the ninth president, caught a cold while delivering his inaugural address in a rainstorm. He developed pneumonia and died only one month into his term. He was a very brave soldier and a national hero. Can you help Harrison find his "Whale Oil Lamp"?

What's the difference?

John Tyler was the tenth American president. He was the first vice president to succeed a president who died in office. Many in the government wanted him known only as an "acting president." He disagreed—he was the president! In fact, he wouldn't accept mail addressed to the "acting president." Circle 10 things in the bottom drawing that are different from the top one.

Find the way to riches!

James Knox Polk was the eleventh president. During his time in office the country went through a period of "western expansion." When gold was discovered in California, the great "Gold Rush" began. Polk went to war with Mexico and we won California. Help President Polk find his way to California and get his hands on some of that gold!

What doesn't belong here?

Zachary Taylor, the twelfth president, was a career soldier before he was president. His war horse was named "Old Whitey." Old Whitey was allowed to graze on the White House lawn. Find and circle 10 things that don't belong in the picture above.

Can you find ten books?

The thirteenth president was Millard Fillmore. While Fillmore was in office, Harriet Beecher Stowe wrote the popular book *Uncle Tom's Cabin*. Find and circle 10 books hidden in the picture.

Where are the ballots?

Franklin Pierce, the fourteenth president, fought in the Mexican-American war. He served as president from 1853 to 1857. In this picture he is trying to get votes. Find and circle 10 ballots hidden in this picture.

What's missing down on the farm?

James Buchanan, the fifteenth president, grew up on a farm in Pennsylvania. After his term as president, he returned to his home. Find and circle 10 things in the right picture that are different from the left.

Who and what don't belong?

On November 19, 1863, at the dedication of a soldier's cemetery in Gettysburg, Pennsylvania—four and a half months after one of the most horrible battles of the Civil War—Abraham Lincoln, the sixteenth president, gave his Gettysburg Address. Can you find 16 things or people that don't belong in the crowd scene?

WOW!

Andrew Johnson was the seventeenth American president. Here we find him about to deliver a speech before a very odd crowd. Find and circle 17 things that don't belong in this picture.

Where are they?

The eighteenth president, Ulysses S. Grant, was a war hero of the Civil War. In this picture, he is shown at a tea party with some of his soldiers—but he has lost his fork, knife, and spoon. Find and circle them.

What's the difference?

Rutherford B. Hayes, the nineteenth president, fought gallantly during the Civil War. Later on, he won a close presidential race. After his term in office, he spent a good deal of time improving the school system. Find and circle 10 things in the bottom picture that are different from the top one.

Find the way to the library!

James A. Garfield, the twentieth president, was born in a log cabin. In his lifetime he was a scholar, a lawyer, a senator, a Civil War hero, and president of the United States! He also loved to read books. Can you help him find his way to the local library?

What's missing in the picture?

President Chester A. Arthur was the twenty-first president. He was a greatly respected figure. Here we see the president out shopping, list in hand. Find and circle 10 things in the bottom picture that are different from the top one.

What's missing at the polls?

Grover Cleveland was the twenty-second and the twenty-fourth president! He is the only president to have been elected to two non-consecutive terms. In this picture he is voting at the polls. Find and circle 6 things in the bottom picture that are different from the top one.

Where's the lost apple?

Benjamin Harrison, the twenty-third president, is having a party for his pet goat, "Old Whiskers." It certainly is a mixed crowd! The president misplaced an apple for Old Whiskers. Can you find it?

Find the pencil.

Remember the Maine

William McKinley was the twenty-fifth president. The Spanish-American war started during his term in office. The battleship *USS Maine* blew up in Havana, Cuba, on February 15, 1898.

The president is displaying a poster that shows the *Maine* before it was destroyed. The phrase "Remember the Maine" was a popular war slogan. Find a pencil hidden in the picture above, which the president can use to sign autographs.

What's missing?

Theodore Roosevelt, the twenty-sixth president, was the youngest president to take office. He led the Rough Riders in the Spanish-American War and became a hero. Find and circle 10 items in the bottom picture that are different from the top one.

What's missing?

[See pages 28–29 for President William H. Taft.]

Woodrow Wilson, the twenty-eighth president, wanted peace, but during his term in office he entered World War I. He wanted a League of Nations after the war, but Congress voted against joining. Find and circle 10 things in the picture on the right that are different from the left one.

Find the hidden items.

The twenty-seventh president, William H. Taft, always said he was more of a lawyer than a politician. His goal in life was to be the Chief Justice of the Supreme Court. He accomplished this goal in 1921.

In this picture, President Taft is giving a speech to a large, noisy crowd of people. There are 5 items hidden in this picture. Find and circle a pencil, book, mirror, ruler, and judge's gavel.

Where are the teapots?

President Warren G. Harding was the twenty-ninth American president. Harding's presidential term was full of scandals, including his involvement in the Teapot Dome oil-field fraud in Wyoming.

This picture shows President and Mrs. Harding moving into the White House in 1921. Find and circle 10 of their missing teapots.

Connect the dots!

Calvin Coolidge was the thirtieth president. He was a man of few words and known to be frugal. His birthday is on the fourth of July, Independence Day. Connect the dots to see what's in the picture that President Coolidge is holding.

Draw the lines.

36

38

37

35

[See pages 34–35 for Presidents Eisenhower, Roosevelt, Hoover, and Truman.] Here are John F. Kennedy, Lyndon B. Johnson, Richard M. Nixon, and Gerald R. Ford. Draw a line from the number on the left, identifying each president's order in office, to the correct face on the right.

Put the presidents in order.

31

32

Here are Dwight D. Eisenhower, Franklin D. Roosevelt, Herbert Hoover, and Harry S. Truman. They are not in the right order.

33

34

To put them in the right order, choose one of the numbers listed and write it under the president to whom it belongs. Do this for each president.

The Obamas move in.

[See page 38 for Presidents Bush, Reagan, and Carter.]
President Bill Clinton, the forty-second president, and President George W. Bush, our forty-third president, moved out of the White House when their terms were over.

Now, the forty-fourth president, Barack Obama, lives there with his family. This picture shows the Obamas on move-in day. Find and circle two airline tickets, a basketball, a puppy, a diary, two cell phones, and a hairbrush.

Put the balloons in order.

39 40 41

Here are George H. W. Bush, Ronald Reagan, and Jimmy Carter. Put them in order by writing the correct number on the line next to each president.

Solutions

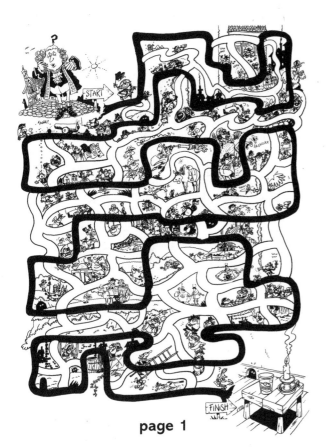

page 1

page 2

page 3

page 4

page 5

page 6

page 7

page 8

page 9

page 10

page 11

page 12

page 13

page 14

page 15

page 16

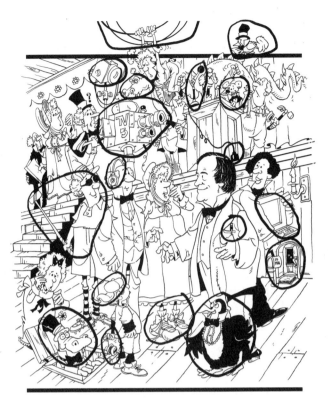

page 17

page 18

page 19

page 20

page 21

page 22

page 23

pages 24–25

page 26

page 27

pages 28–29

pages 30–31

page 32

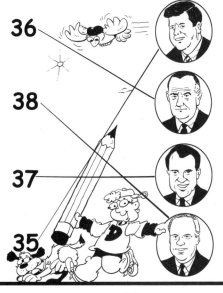

page 33

34 31
33 32
31 33
32 34

pages 34–35

pages 36–37

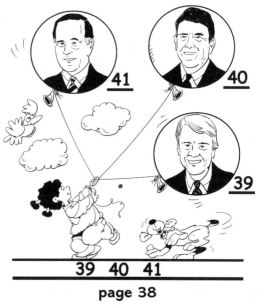

41
40
39

39 40 41

page 38